The Shower, the Course & the Thought Bubble

the SHOWER, the COURSE & the THOUGHT BUBBLE

Rum Charles

Published by Brolga Publishing Pty Ltd
ABN 46 063 962 443
PO Box 12544
A'Beckett St
Melbourne, VIC, 8006
Australia
email: markzocchi@brolgapublishing.com.au

All rights reserved. No part of this publication may be reproduced, stored in a retrieval system or transmitted in any form or by any means electronic, mechanical, photocopying, recording or otherwise without prior permission from the publisher.

All original photos and artwork included in this book are the property of the author and used with permission.

Copyright © Rum Charles

National Library of Australia Cataloguing-in-Publication data
Author: Charles, Rum.
Title: The shower, the course and the thought
                bubble / Rum Charles.
ISBN: 9781921221941 (pbk.)
Subjects: Success in business.
                Success.
Dewey Number: 650.13

Printed in China
Cover Image by Pauline Matthewman
Cover Design by David Khan
Illustrations by Pauline Matthewman
Original edit by Marti Cuatt
Typeset and designed by Diana Evans

a note from Rum Charles

I would like to give my sincere thanks to many people for their assistance and encouragement in getting this book off the ground, including:

Marti Cuatt for the first edit and many, many other things to help get this book published.

Pauline Matthewman for working for me for many years and allowing me the space to write.

John Charles, my brother, for writing a book some 20 years ago and giving me brotherly inspiration.

Rachal Van Wyk, also known as Radical Rachal, for being in the office and taking care of things.

Sue Leeuwenburg for listening to me.

Solomon and Vanessa Charles for being my Children and loving having a crazy Dad.

And every single person who I have ever had the pleasure of being in a training room or seminar with. In some way or other you are all in this book.

CONTENTS

Foreword 11
EQUAL is born 13

Part 1 – E 17

Part 2 – Q 33

Part 3 – U 63

Part 4 – A 81

Part 5 – L 101

Part 6 – EQUAL 121

the Shower, the Course & the Thought Bubble

About the Author

London-born Rum Charles is the founder and principal consultant of Indigo Training. He is a vibrant, passionate and dynamic facilitator who specialises in training across a broad spectrum of topics, especially during times change and during the introduction of new technologies.

Rum began his working life in sales, before becoming a commodities broker in the UK, where he earned enough money to begin what became extensive travels.

He settled in Melbourne 16 years ago and soon established Indigo Training after being inundated by requests from organisations to train their sales staff (including the Australian Football League and Drake Training, to name but two).

Rum facilitates and trains people with same

passion and integrity by which he lives his life, encouraging participants to become fully involved in the learning process through engaging them in real life scenarios to reach training goals and integrate the principles learned throughout their whole lives.

the Shower, the Course & the Thought Bubble

FOREWORD

This is a self-help book that utilises a philosophy that guides you through five very simple steps to teach you the art of effective communication.

Communication is at the core of almost every daily activity, so it's important that we know how to do it effectively. It is a process of receiving information, letting it make sense, then returning the information – through finding out more or taking a course of action.

Even though this core activity is central to our lives, it is amazing how ineffective many of us are as communicators. This is where EQUAL will help.

Written through the eyes of well known training facilitator, Rum Charles, *The Shower, The Course and The Thought Bubble* takes us to a training room in need of a bit of oomph – and how the principle evolved through simply testing it out.

Since that first day of EQUAL thirteen years ago, the philosophy has been employed as the centrepiece of every Indigo Training Program that Rum Charles and his team of talented facilitators conducts. Time and again he receives emails, letters and phone calls telling him how it has changed people's lives, and therefore is changing the world for the better, one person at a time.

the Shower, the Course & the Thought Bubble

EQUAL is born
(or beamed directly to Rum's consciousness)

What is EQUAL and how has EQUAL changed my life and the lives of others?

Well, there I was standing in the shower (sorry for the mental image), soaking up the positive vibes created by the negatively charged ions, when all of a sudden it hit me like a bolt out of the blue.

"My God", I thought. "No that cannot be! It's way too simple, how can that be so?!"

As I stood there allowing this very simple thought to run around my brain, looking for the holes, it became obvious.

"I know, I'll use it in a training room, and allow all the course participants to show me how this very simple idea could not possibly work."

the Shower, the Course & the Thought Bubble

With that, I got out of the shower.[1] (It's at this point I must apologise to Melbourne Water, because 25 minute showers are definitely not a good idea.)

A few hours later, there I was, standing in a room full of participants conducting a Customer Service course, or something along those lines. You know the type of thing – ten people, all from different companies and all with different needs, wants and objectives and for the most part not happy to be there in the first place.

We were about halfway through day two of the course, following the standard Customer Service 101 manual. Eyes were glazing over, heads were nodding and bodies were stealing all the remaining energy to digest lunch, leaving brains to fend for themselves.

The course had hit the Doldrums. (For those of you who don't know, the Doldrums are a real place, between five degrees north and five degrees

---

1. All this began on a cold October morning at 6.48 am, in the year… Well, sometime in the mid nineties when Melbourne still had plenty of water and no water restrictions.

south of the equator. You can't give the Doldrums a precise location because they shift, depending on how the universe feels about our planet on any given day. The Doldrums are a totally becalmed stretch of ocean, feared by all mariners in the days of sail. Strangely enough, the Doldrums are also the source of all the worlds' winds (except perhaps for my Great Aunt Mabel, who creates cyclones of immense power inside her own intestinal tract).

What was I to do? The course was in danger of being overtaken by lethargy, closely followed by despondency and then being dashed on the rocks of boredom – a sure way to sink any fledgling training career.

I had to whip up a storm! Something new, something controversial, something to be challenged, and something to boil the blood of this lacklustre, motley crew.

I did a mental search of my armoury, tossing aside cutlasses, bludgeons, muskets, and shot, and then my mind's eye fell upon EQUAL,

the Shower, the Course & the Thought Bubble

"Aha![2]" I thought, eyeing the crew in front of me. "Here's my chance to kill two birds with one stone, put some wind back in the sails of the course and dispel this crazy, simplistic notion from my mind!"

---

2. That Aha was worthy of "International talk like a pirate day" usually held in September.
http://www.talklikeapirate.com/

the Shower, the Course & the Thought Bubble

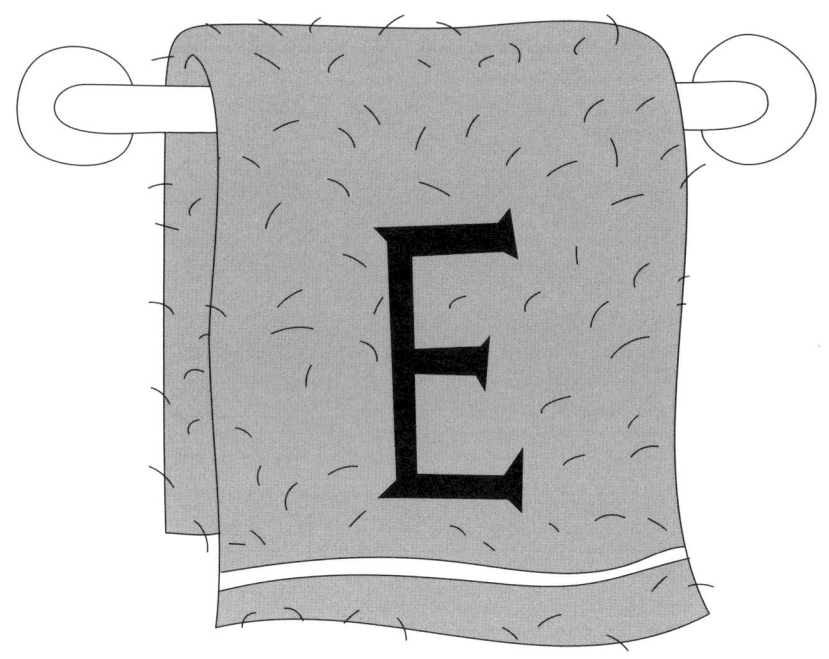

the Shower, the Course & the Thought Bubble

the Shower, the Course & the Thought Bubble

part ONE

Inspired by the thought of moving the course out of the Doldrums and doing my own market research, I grabbed the closest whiteboard marker, which just happened to be purple, and scrawled the following upon the whiteboard:

the Shower, the Course & the Thought Bubble

As I turned to face the group I was encouraged, but also a little bemused, to see amongst the faces two wry smiles and a look of shock.

"Movement!" I thought.

I wasn't quite sure where the movement was going, but there was definitely movement. To capitalise on this slight breeze, I asked a question.

"What do you think the E on the board might stand for?"

At this point the wry smiles turned to broad grins and the look of shock to one of horror.

the Shower, the Course & the Thought Bubble

After a quick but heated discussion on the use and dangers of non-prescribed pharmaceuticals, which had the marked side effect of waking most of the group from their post lunch digestive slump, I again asked the question: "So … what do you think the E on the board might stand for?"

As the group shouted out every word beginning with E they could think of (including 'every'), I realised that EQUAL had passed its first test.

The letter E, thanks to popular culture, is now a contentious letter; therefore, by writing it on a whiteboard, I had created a great PIS[3] for EQUAL.

---

3. PIS: Powerful Impact Statement. Any new concept or idea must have one of these to get anywhere

the Shower, the Course & the Thought Bubble

Eventually I heard what I was waiting for. A quiet woman at the back of the room uttered the word with as much disinterest as she could muster.

"Empaaathy…" she sighed.

"Did you mean empathy?" I asked, suddenly aware of her long drawn out tone.

"Yeahhhh…" she said.

I turned to face her, safe in the knowledge that anyone this negative would know just how to dispel this crazy notion from my mind.

"What does empathy mean?" I asked her.

"To put yourself in someone else's shoes," she replied. "Which of course is impossible, as 'I am me' and 'they are them', so how can I be them? It's not possible, is it?"

Vindicated, I thought, "scrap EQUAL and get back to the 101 manual".

Then, from the left side of the room, I heard a voice say, "Yes it is!"

"What do you mean?" I enquired, turning to face the voice.

"Well," the voice went on, "there has to be two 'yous', one which is your normal you, and a neutral you!"

At this point everyone in the room looked totally confused, including me.

The voice went on. "No, no… you stay one person, but it's not about you, it's about them," now looking directly at me, pleading for some kind of recognition or understanding, and as he did so, a volcano erupted in my head.

the Shower, the Course & the Thought Bubble

"Yes… yes," I said. "I do understand!"

I turned back to the whiteboard and wrote[4]:

4. Thanks to the proliferation of mobile phones with SMS, 'U' can now mean you. Awful but true.

the Shower, the Course & the Thought Bubble

"You are both right," I said, addressing 'Ms Negative' and 'The Voice'. "No-one can be anyone else, but we can open ourselves up and put our own experiences and feeling towards the person and/or situation on hold."

"In most cases, everything we see and hear is filtered through the experiences of our own lives, therefore we respond with an EGO-driven answer. When we respond in this way we set ourselves up for disappointment or miscommunication. We do it all the time."

"What do you mean?" asked a guy wearing an expensive suit, looking up from his impossibly small techno toy.

"Well," I went on, "people say things like, 'if I were her, I would not do it like that, I would do it like X' or 'if I were him, I'd be able to do X much better than that."

Both of these statements are fundamentally flawed. If you were them, you would do it exactly as they were doing it, because you would be them, hence:

I is not U

I is I and U is U."

The suit with the techno toy eyed me with a mixture of suspicion and scepticism, implying I was fine as long as I stayed well away from him. I continued anyway.

"So going back to having two yous… two yous gives us a double you (W), and if we put a W in front of EGO, we get WE/GO not EGO. By removing our ego we can, in effect, remove the filters of our own mind and become a neutral listener – listening, in reality, to what the other person is actually saying," I said, and then took a breath before continuing.

the Shower, the Course & the Thought Bubble

"By communicating without ego, we can be empathetic. It takes courage to be in the world without ego, as it leaves our IDD exposed (The IDD being our inner selves, our inner child)."

This is cool, I thought. Nothing like a bit of Jung in the afternoon. I turned to the group. "Do you get it?" I enquired, feeling somewhat pleased with my own revelation.

Blank… except for a tiny giggle.

the Shower, the Course & the Thought Bubble

"What's so funny?" I asked.

Still giggling, the answer came. "Well, it's like being a mum isn't it?"

"What?" I replied, feeling more than a little insulted. "Go on…"

"It's obvious really. If I got upset and took it personally every time my two-year old banged her fists on my legs telling me she hates me and wished I wasn't her mother, I'd spend most of my time on the floor a blubbering wreck," she began.

"But I know she doesn't really hate me, she's just frustrated with the situation. So as the grown up, I rise above her words and deal with the situation. Five minutes later, she's all smiles and 'I love you mummy!' That's what you're saying, isn't it? Be a grown up and don't take it all so personally. Get over it and deal with the situation in its reality."

28

Feeling somewhat embarrassed at the brilliance and simplicity of her explanation I spluttered, "Yes, spot on! Don't take it personally, take it professionally."

The entire group nodded their understanding, and those who had children gave a knowing giggle of their own.

the Shower, the Course & the Thought Bubble

note to readers: EMPATHY

Mastering empathy is the first step in becoming an effective communicator – and it applies in all aspects of your life.

Using emotional intelligence and being empathetic gives us the capacity to react to the true situation at hand, not merely the emotion being placed in front of us.

The trick to mastering empathy is to let go of the ego and become a neutral listener. That way we can put ourselves in other people's shoes – to listen to their meaning, not apply our own meaning to what they're saying.

By doing this, we are employing our emotional intelligence (which will be covered in a later chapter) in each and every communication with others.

In other words, we need to be in control of our

own emotional responses in order to gain empathy and remain in control of a given situation instead of allowing a situation to be created whereby we can be manipulated.

the Shower, the Course & the Thought Bubble

the Shower, the Course & the Thought Bubble

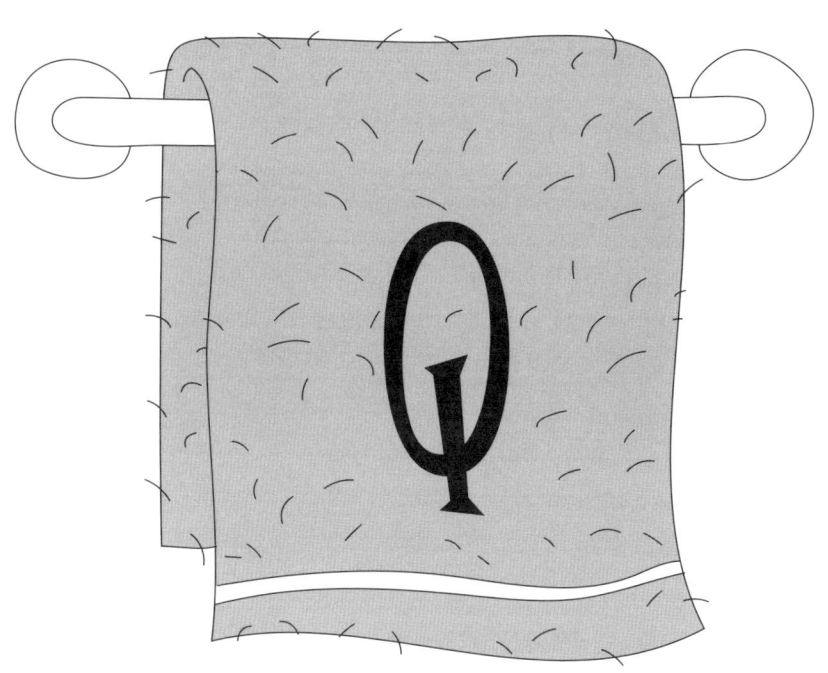

the Shower, the Course & the Thought Bubble

the Shower, the Course & the Thought Bubble

Under the E on the whiteboard I wrote the letter Q and asked this question:

"What is the fastest and best way to get to the reality of the situation, as far as the person you are

the Shower, the Course & the Thought Bubble

dealing with sees it?"

As one, the group shouted:

"QUESTIONS!"

Even Ms Negative and the Expensive Suit Guy (minus techno toy) had joined in on the shout. The Good Ship Training had indeed left the Doldrums, and with a good wind at our backs we were once again under full sail. EQUAL was looking promising!

"There are two types of question…"

"Yeah, Yeah… open and closed. Everybody knows that!" said a small guy with a receding hairline.

the Shower, the Course & the Thought Bubble

It took only one glance to see that he was in sales, and had been for many years. He was the epitome of the eighties-era salesman.

"Ok," I continued, "would you do us the honour of explaining open and closed questions?"

"Why?" he said. "We all know it."

"I don't!" came a sweet voice from the centre of the room.

The eighties-era salesman now focused on a young woman around nineteen years of age with an impressive mane. She was small of stature but had a real presence, and by the look of her, a cutting wit.

Eighties Man flashed his best 'hi there' smile and said, "well for you, I'll explain," and taking a deep breath, he began.

"You see, open questions require an answer you can't just say yes or no to. That's an open question. Closed questions require a yes or no answer, and that's it," he stated.

He looked at her beaming an expectant grin and waited for her to fall at his feet, declaring him the fountain of all wisdom and knowledge, ready to offer herself to him.

Noting the leer in his eyes, her reply was short, sharp, and to the point. "As an answer, it's small and very unsatisfying." And with a quick flick of her impressive mane, not only dismissed the answer, but put Eighties Man back in his box.

She turned, faced me and said, "Is that really it? Just that?"

"No," I said. "I think there is more to it than that!"

"Like what?" flared Eighties man, sensing his

best smile and quick explanation had not won him the fair maiden.

I continued, "well, what words do you think start open questions?"

Quick as a flash, eighties man started to chant, "where, when, how, er, er, er,"

Looking up and feeling kind of silly, he admitted that he knew there were more words, but it had been so long since he'd been made to do the basics, he couldn't remember the rest.

"Anyone else?" I enquired.

Ms Negative remembering that she was naturally negative sighed out, "Whaaat," then retreated.

"Yes! What is a great one!"

Surprised at my enthusiasm for the word 'what' Ms Negative decided to stay engaged in the session.

"Anyone else?"

Broad Grin two tentatively put one forward, "Can?"

"I like it, but… no," I said, to which Broad Grin one said,

"Why?"

"YES!" I said.

"Why can be used to start an open question, but I will put Why in red (red for stop), with a question mark."

"Why?" she asked again.

"Well…" I said looking around the room where I spied a timid guy so hunched over that if you were not looking for him, you would miss him altogether.

I turned to him and asked him to ask Broad Grin one any question he liked as long as it began with Why.

After a little coaching and reassurance that all would be well, he asked: "Why did you choose to wear that skirt today?"

the Shower, the Course & the Thought Bubble

Broad Grin one was immediately taken aback.

"Because it goes with my shoes!" She snapped back, looking all indignant.

"Stop right there," I said. "What just happened?"

Before I could say another word, Timid Guy was now on his feet and across the other side of the room apologising profusely for upsetting Broad Grin one. I asked him what he was apologising for.

"Because I upset her by asking about her skirt!" He said. "It was a stupid thing to say, I don't know why I said it, it just came out!"

I reassured him that it had nothing to do with the skirt, and in fact it did not matter what he asked, the reaction would have been the same.

"I get it," said The Voice, "it does not matter what you say after the word why, because no one is really listening. All they hear is that you are attacking them!"

"Spot on." I said "Why is aggressive and puts people on the defensive straight away."

"But you said you had to get to the root of the issue," chimed in Eighties Man, "and knowing why is the root, isn't it?"

Whenever you are tempted to use the word 'why', simply substitute it for the word 'what' and frame your question around that word instead, and I promise you, your communications will be far more favourable.

Eighties Man immediately turned to the young woman and said, "Why don't you and I go out tonight?"

Before she could answer he leaned in close to her and crooned, "What you doing tonight babe?"

At that, the young woman fixed Eighties Man

with a withering gaze and replied, "I'm washing my hair."

Then she looked up and said, "I understand that even though the question was phrased more positively the second time around, it still does not guarantee a positive response. For example, it does not matter how an aging, balding, short, unattractive man asks me out – I will always have something better to do, even if it is watching paint dry."

"Exactly" I said. "Individual choice is still very relevant."

the Shower, the Course & the Thought Bubble

At this point all the participants burst out laughing and Eighties Man shrank into his chair.

"Okay, okay, let's continue. So far we have five words that start open questions: where, what, how, when and why. There are two more. Any takers?"

"Can?" No sorry, closed.

"Will?" No sorry, closed.

"Is?" No sorry, closed.

"Let me give you a clue," I said. "How many incarnations hang out with a girl called Rose in the TARDIS[5]?"

"Who, yes Doctor Who! The word you want is who, it is, isn't it?"

I looked towards the back of the room to see a massive smile on the face of a woman in her mid twenties. She looked back at me beaming and held up a bag with the word SMEG[6] splashed across it.

---

5. TARDIS stands for Time And Relative Dimensions In Space, by the way.
6. For all you non sci-fi people out there the word Smeg, or better still Smeghead, is Dave Lister's favourite insult – Dave lister being the last human being alive in the galaxy. In fact he is caught in a temporal loop ensuring the survival of the human race. See BBC drama Red Dwarf.

As I looked at the bag I was more than sure that the word smeg had nothing to do with kitchen appliances in this context.

"Yes," I said. 'Who' is the word I was looking for."

"I knew it," she beamed again. "All things sci- fi, that's me. Once you put it like that I knew I would get it."

"Well here's another one for you. Not quite sci-fi but have a go anyway," I responded. "Comes out on 31 October, rides a broomstick, and some would say is their mother-in-law."

Quick as a flash Eighties Man leapt to his feet.

"Old hag? No! No! I mean witch."

At this point he suddenly realised that all eyes were upon him, so looking somewhat sheepish he sat down and explained that it is a different spelling, of course.

"Thanks," I said. "You're right, the word I am looking for is w-h-i-c-h. Which not w-i-t-c-h." "Through the correct use of these seven words we can greatly improve our communications, as open questions give us *information in conversation.*"

All eyes were on me, so I continued.

"Information in conversation is a powerful thing. It can seem as though you are having an ordinary conversation with someone but what you are in fact doing is gathering all the information you need to respond to any given situation. Through the use of open questions you will be able to get to the root of the issue."

"Open questions open up the conversation while closed questions close the conversation down. What words do you believe start closed questions?"

the Shower, the Course & the Thought Bubble

"Can, will and is," stated Broad Grin two with an especially broad grin.

"Well done," I said. "Good to see your memory is still intact."

"Are," said the Shy Guy, feeling somewhat better about himself after the explanation for why had been given.

"Thanks!" I said in my most encouraging tone.

Then I heard the word 'do' and looked around, pleased to see the guy in the expensive suit had well and truly put his techno toy away and seemed to be quite enjoying himself in the company of other humans. A rare event I believe.

"Thanks! Do is most definitely a closed question. Past tense of do?" I asked, looking to motivate

the Shower, the Course & the Thought Bubble

others to contribute.

"Done," said The Voice.

"Umm." I responded. "The past tense of 'do' is in fact 'did' rather than done. Don't worry, I once asked a group of librarians the same question and got the same answer – 'done'."

"Any more?" I asked, knowing full well that there were plenty. "Okay, I'll give you a clue." I wrote the letters o-u-l-d on the board three times and invited people to add a letter or letters to get the answer.

"Could" said Broad Grin One, not to be outdone by Broad Grin Two in the memory stakes, as they seemed to have formed quite a bond.

I wrote 'could' on the board and as I turned there was Eighties Man with a smile he thought no one could see thinking 'wood' and saying 'would'. I ignored the innuendo and wrote 'would' on the board.

As I looked around waiting for the last "o-u-l-d" to be filled I heard:

"I should have got it ages ago! It's should, isn't

it?" called out The Voice with a triumphant note.

"Yes." I said, "Should. One of my least favoured words of all time."

"What's wrong with it?" asked The Voice.

"Well as far as I can see, we use it in three ways on ourselves and they're all negative." I began.

"The first way we use it is to talk ourselves out of doing things we actually want to do, like going to the gym. You know what it's like, you get home from work, slump into a chair and say to yourself or whoever you live with 'I should go to the gym', 'I should really go to the gym', 'I really should go to the gym'. Once you have said should in this context three times you know darn well that you are no longer going to the gym."

"It's this negative self-talk, along with the fact you have now had a cup of tea and a Tim Tam that stops you from going, as everyone knows you can't possibly go to the gym now. You can't go working out on a full tummy, can you?"

"What should we say then?" asked the young

woman with the impressive mane.

"Next time this happens, simply replace the word should with will. 'I will go to the gym!' and see what happens."

"Ok," she said. "I'll give it a go, and no Tim Tams until I get back after a good solid workout!"

"The next way we use it against ourselves is to beat ourselves up about something that has already happened: 'I should have done this', or 'I should have done that' I should have gone to the gym etcetera, etcetera," I continued.

"Well there is no use berating ourselves about something that cannot be changed, instead it is far better to accept that the past has happened, but know we can control our future. So instead of saying 'I should have', try saying 'next time I will'."

"That's a little simplistic," said Ms Negative.

(I noticed her tone was by now lighter and her words were less drawn out. Could this be engagement? I thought to myself.)

But before I could formulate a response, Sci-fi

the Shower, the Course & the Thought Bubble

Girl jumped in and said, "And so is breathing, but it keeps me alive."

"I used to be like that, always down on myself about what I was or wasn't eating, or what I was wearing and how I didn't fit in with the other 'normal' girls, but once I decided to be me and started looking forwards and not backwards it all changed. I am happy to be me now and take each day and each person as it or they come. No more 'I should be this or that' for me." At that, Ms Negative suddenly looked thoughtful and slightly wistful.

the Shower, the Course & the Thought Bubble

I continued, "and lastly we use should against each other. 'You should get a hair cut, you should get out more, you should see a doctor etcetera, etcetera, but each time we do this to someone they are forced by their nature – their human nature – to defend themselves, usually by holding their position on whatever the topic or action may be."

"So how do you help someone or tell someone off?" asked the woman with the two and twelve year old kids. "If I did not tell my twelve year old she should clean her room, her clothes would live on the floor forever. Where would that get anyone?"

"When you tell her to clean her room in that manner, how good a job does she do?" I ventured.

"Lousy! She picks up a few things, puts them

in a drawer or two, then scurries off out with her friends and I'm left to sort the clean from the dirty and put things away properly," she replied.

"On the rare occasions that she actually decides to clean her room for herself, what kind of job does she do then?" I asked.

"Oh fantastic. The floors are washed, all the carpets are vacuumed, everything is put away and once I even saw her dusting!" she responded.

"So what does that tell you?" I queried.

"Oh my god!" she said. "I stop her from cleaning her room. I tell her she should clean her room almost every day, but if I eased up a bit she would be happy to do it."

"That, and she has you sooo sucked in," said Broad Grin One. "She knows that every time you say you 'should' clean your room, you are going to do it for her so why bother."

"That's it. No more 'should' for me!" said the woman with the twelve year old. "And I'll also stop telling her dad he 'should' go to the doctor. I'll just tell him that we love him and don't want him to die, that and it won't hurt. That'll get him off his arse."

"Ok, so there we have it," I said. "*Open and closed questions* have been around forever, so used correctly they can change your communications with customers, co-workers, family, friends, enemies – anyone. Also note that by asking questions you gain control of the conversation. Whoever is asking the questions is in control of the conversation."

"There's one more thing to remember about asking questions, which is possibly the most important and most difficult thing of all. What do you think it might be?" I said and then I paused.

I lowered my energy level, and thus the energy in the room, and waited.

There was a gaping hole in the room as people thought about the question, then after about twenty seconds (which felt more like twenty minutes) Eighties Man blurted out in a loud voice, "I give up, we don't know! Tell us."

I thought about his language for a moment. 'I

give up, WE don't know'.

Strange how his decision was now not his own, but he had claimed this for the rest of the group as well as himself without consultation. Oh how he feared being separated from the herd.

I pulled myself back from this distraction, waited a second or two longer then continued.

"SILENCE IS YOUR GOLDEN TOOL"

"When you ask a question, the most important thing to remember is to…" I turned to the white board and wrote 'SHUT THE F#*@ UP'.

I turned around to see Broad Grin One smirking away at Broad Grin Two and kept on talking.

"Not a word. After all if you want to know the answer to the question, then wait. Now this can be painful, as we have just experienced. When nothing is happening and we are waiting, time suddenly slows down and each second seems to feel like a minute," I said.

(Time is not linear; in fact time is a construct of the human mind and can be bent or altered depending on our attitudinal state.)

I kept going. "Some people who do not want to answer your questions have become experts in not saying anything. They will simply try to outwait you, hoping you will speak first so they can distract you into another conversation. Then they do not have to answer the original question. Teenagers (and politicians) have this down to a fine art."

"Tell me about it" said The Voice. "The seventeen-year-old in my house is an expert at this technique. I ask her where she's been until one o'clock in the morning and I get nothing. Just that look. So I get angry and yell at her to go to bed and think hard about the worry she has put her mother and I through and she just smiles and goes off to bed." He was clearly frustrated.

"So we never get to find out where she's been or what she's been doing, as in the morning – I say morning but it's more like early afternoon – she's all smiles and apologies, telling us she understands and how sorry she is, and we leave it at that."

the Shower, the Course & the Thought Bubble

By this time The Voice's light bulb was well and truly on. "I have never thought of myself as easily manipulated but obviously I am. Boy is she in for a shock the next time she's home late. I'll take a seat in front of her door, ask the question and..."

Before he could say the words the group, including Ms Negative I was pleased to see, all shouted out in unison "SHUT THE FUCK UP".

It was at this point the trainer from the next

room knocked on my door and asked us to keep the noise down. I decided to break for afternoon tea and do some apologising of my own. As I was apologising, the other facilitator just looked at me and said, "I don't know what you're doing in there but it's working. I wish I could get my group to be as animated as your lot."

"Thanks," I said and inwardly smiled, as EQUAL had just passed another hurdle. Maybe, just maybe, this EQUAL thing might work.

I went for my afternoon walk and chocolate bar[7].

---

7. Chocolate – a real delicacy – was first introduced into Europe by the Spanish during conquest of Mexico in the 1500s. It was taken as a beverage, however because of its bitterness, sugar and cinnamon were added to make it more palatable. Due to the high cost of sugar and cacao, chocolate was only available to the very wealthy. In France, for example, the drink was only available to members of the royal court. It remained a luxury beverage until the 1800s, when, with industrialisation, it became available to the masses in block form.

note to readers: QUESTIONS

Many of us don't ask questions because we're concerned that others may think of us as ignorant or uninformed. The opposite is true – it is fine not to understand something initially and to ask for clarification, which is the only way to gain real understanding of a situation.

In order to ask questions, you need to be assertive (as opposed to aggressive). Assertiveness is a product of emotional intelligence, covered in the next chapter.

Asking questions is also a creative process. When someone is speaking, ensure you remain silent, which enables you to listen (as opposed to hear – which is just being aware of noises whizzing past your ears).

Being still and silent allows us to internalise the words being spoken and find context within the conversation, thus ensuring you do not mis-hear the message. You then gain the information you need as well as further empathy about the situation or other person's emotional state, which enables you to formulate the next question before asking it in the context of the communication.

Remember too, the different types of questions. Open questions start conversations and closed questions tend to close conversations and be one word answers. However closed questions can be a powerful tool for gaining commitment. But be careful with why, which can be interpreted as an aggressive open question and put the other person in a defensive position.

the Shower, the Course & the Thought Bubble

Open	Closed
How	Is
What	Would
Where	Could
When	Can
Which	Will
Who	Did
Why	Have
(but be careful when using)	

Remember: Open questions give **information in conversation** and closed questions gain **commitment**.

And the golden rule: once you've asked the question, shut the F#*@ up and listen to the answer.

the Shower, the Course & the Thought Bubble

the Shower, the Course & the Thought Bubble

the Shower, the Course & the Thought Bubble

part THREE

"Everyone back?" I asked as I closed the door. I looked around the room – all accounted for.

"How was your break?" I asked.

"Great," said The Voice. "We were talking about kids and how easily they have learned to manipulate us and how this relates back to the workplace. You know, most people learn their communication skills at home in the first five or six years of their life, then use variations on those themes in their adult communications, especially in the work place," The Voice ventured.

"Why do… I mean, what makes you say that?" asked the Shy Guy, sounding much less shy now.

"Well…" The Voice continued, "I reckon we spend more awake time with our co-workers than we do with the people we live with and so after a while we let down our façade and be ourselves – manipulations, hang ups and all."

What do you think?" he said, turning to me.

"I think you're right," I replied. "Most people communicate from an emotional standpoint, which is based around how they perceive the situation in relation to what they want to get out of it, or from a defensive position. But what we are talking about here is moving beyond this child-like communication and into something much more meaningful, and above all, mature."

It was time to ask a question. "Has anyone ever heard of something called E-I, or Emotional Intelligence?"

"I've heard of A-I," said Sci-fi girl. "Artificial Intelligence and a great movie, the whole movie was done using CGI, or computer generated images. Really cool stuff! That movie is all about emotions and their reality."

"Not quite what I was looking for" I said.

"Emotional Intelligence…"

I wrote a big U under the E and Q.

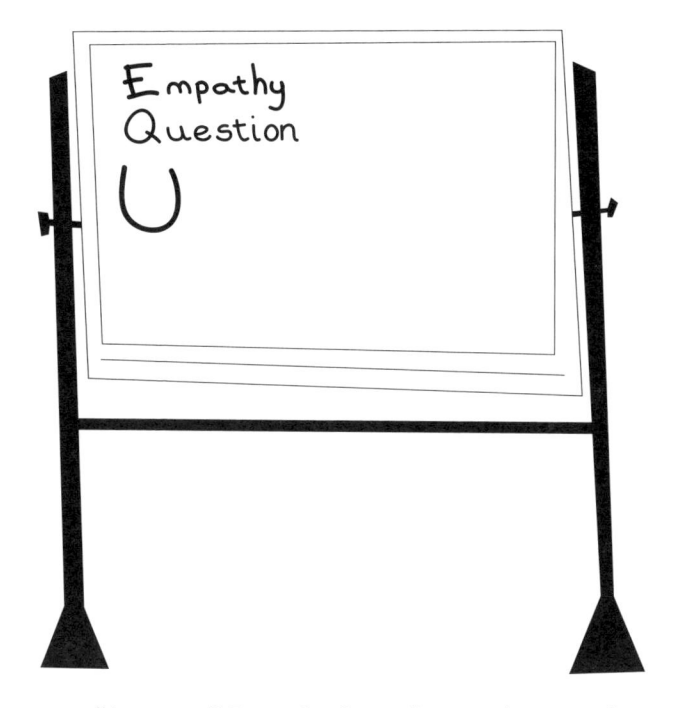

```
Empathy
Question
U
```

"Anyone?" I was looking for another word.

"Understanding?" ventured the young woman with the impressive mane.

"Yes." I responded. "It's the ability to understand your own emotions and those of others and use this information for the greater good."

"How do you know what the greater good is?

I mean good is subjective isn't it?" pointed out the Expensive Suit Guy. "I see it all the time. Both sides claim they are speaking for the good of the company, department or whatever, and are really trying to get their own way."

"That's it," I replied with enthusiasm. "Remember in Empathy it's about being a grown up and seeing the bigger picture. That's emotional intelligence: controlling yourself and stepping back to look at the bigger picture while truly listening to the other person or persons you are communicating with."

"There is a world of difference between listening and hearing. Have you ever been at home and had the radio or TV on in the background while you are doing something else?" I asked.

"Yeah, sure I have," piped up Eighties Man. "When me and my ex-Mrs used to be in bed watching TV and I'd be in the mood to give her one we would often do it with the TV on, you know the boring bit of the late news, and I'd still get to watch the sports report!"

An uncomfortable silence descended on the room until the woman with the twelve-year old simply said, "she left you didn't she."

"Yeah, just up and left one day. Didn't even tell me why."

There was a collective shaking of heads. I continued.

"You see it's about being present – not just physically, but emotionally and sometimes spiritually as well. When all these parts of ourselves come together then we are ready to truly listen."

"A lot of the time we think we are listening but really we are just hearing the words and have already decided on our response before the person has even finished their first sentence."

"Or we are so busy being distracted by background noise that the person's message somehow becomes fused with all the other voices, including the little voice in our own heads, therefore we often misinterpret what we think the other person has said."

"So how do you listen then?" asked Miss Negative. "We can't wrap ourselves up in a bubble every time we want to talk to someone."

"No we can't, but have a listen to what you have just said," I replied (very happy her tone had by now lost its practised sigh).

"Merely talking to someone implies either your superiority or that the communication is all one way – your way."

"I believe it is a far more equal communication when we talk with people rather than to them, or to be more accurate still, at them. The key here is to focus. Stop and focus on the person you are communicating with and eliminate as many distractions as possible."

"For example, someone is passing by your desk and while still walking tries to tell you something. Now you may hear their words, but if you are on the phone or deep in thought, replying to an email or anything else, you won't have listened to their message properly. Many times they finish whatever they were saying by saying 'okay', and we reply 'okay', so in their mind they have communicated."

"But the fact is you have no real idea of what they were on about. So what do we do to avoid looking stupid and having to ask again? We guess."

I looked around the room. Everyone was listening.

"Tell me about it," said The Voice. "It happens to me all the time at home. I'm out in the shed working on my boat and my partner walks in, says something and finishes with 'okay love?' And me being the fool that I am simply says 'okay love' back."

the Shower, the Course & the Thought Bubble

"Then," he continued, "the next day I'm in the dog house because I failed to do whatever it was I was supposed to do and my defence is 'you didn't ask me', and she says 'yes I did! I remember it clearly – I went to your shed and asked you and you said 'okay love'."

the Shower, the Course & the Thought Bubble

"So what you're saying is it's more often than not our own fault that we don't understand what people have said to us," chimed in Broad Grin Two.

"Partly," I said.

"Yeah, but how can you say to your boss or manager that you didn't understand what they said? They'll think you are being smart."

"Or an idiot," chipped in Broad Grin One in support of Broad Grin Two.

"Training," I said. "Isn't it up to us to ensure that people communicate with us in a way that we understand? After all how can they know the best way to get a message across to us unless we show them."

"How do you do that?" asked Broad Grin One, although not quite grinning.

"Slow them down and get them to focus by doing it yourself. Don't engage in the **rush of communication**.

"How?" Asked everyone in the room.

"Well…"

"Step 1. Stop whatever you are doing and look the person/s you are communicating with square in the face. This lets them know that you are giving them your full attention."

"Step 2. Pick up a pen and paper to take notes. You'll be amazed at the power of a note pad and pen. People tend to slow their rate of speech to match our speed of note taking and in doing so, think about the words they are using, particularly if they can see you writing their words down."

"Step 3. Paraphrase back to them what they have communicated to you."

"What's paraphrase?" asked Broad Grin One.

"Say it back to them in your own words," responded Sci-fi Girl.

"Way cool, thanks," said Broad Grin One.

I continued. "You can now internalise and understand, then you prove you understand by telling them what they told you. And best of all is…

"Step 4. At the end of the communication you get agreement that all parties understand what has been said."

"Yeah that's fine to say, but managers won't slow down while you write it down and go over it. They all think they are so important and are forever running off to meetings or out to another big lunch appointment," piped up Broad Grin Two.

I turned to face him again and said, "ALL MANAGERS ARE DOGS."

I heard a collective gasp echo around the room.

"Your manager is there to serve you, not the other way around. The job of a manager is to go into battle against other dogs (managers) to protect you, to go out and look for and bring back as many bones (resources) as you need to get your tasks completed, sniff out problems, be loyal and supportive, use their excellent hearing to warn you of what you cannot hear for yourself and to make you feel good when you feel low by always being available and cheerful, just like a good dog," I said.

"However," I went on, "like all dogs your dog

the Shower, the Course & the Thought Bubble

will need training and whose job is it to train your dog?"

"Ours" said Shy Guy (no longer in a shy way).

"And how do you best train a dog?" I asked.

"By kicking it," mumbled Eighties Man, sounding a lot less sure of himself now.

"Same way you train kids" said the woman with the two and twelve-year-old kids. "With consistency. If you always do things the same way with your kids, dogs, and manager they will learn to work with you in your way, as it's easier to do so because they'll know what to expect from dealing with you."

"So at home it's the same deal," said The Voice, "except you don't need to write it down. But what we can do is choose when and where to have important or difficult conversations or ask someone to do something."

"Yes" I answered. "The meal table is a good place (over dinner or just afterwards), as this is a time that people are focused and as you're eating, this will naturally slow the conversation to a good pace," I suggested.

"Time to start having dinner around the table again most nights. I'd forgotten how much we used to talk and laugh at the table," said The Voice.

"Oh," I said. "To answer the original question about what's the greater good, the greater good can only come about when an organisation is engaged in **customer focus** rather than **customer service**. A customer focused organisation involves consistency from every single person in the company making decisions, based on what's best for the customer relationship, not what's best for the managers or departments staff members' egos. What do you think? I asked the guy in the expensive suit

"Makes sense to me," he said.

note to readers: UNDERSTANDING

Think about the amount of times you've taken a certain course of action without fully understanding the situation at hand. Then think about how effective and successful the outcomes have been. Chances are, they would have been far more effective had you gained complete understanding.

It is one of the most important aspects in all parts of your life and is a key part of the EQUAL philosophy.

Real understanding can only be reached through the process of empathising and asking questions to get to a point of view.

It's not simply an intellectual act (that's knowing, which is different from understanding), it is a combination of intellectual, emotional, and to some degree, intuitive understanding.

Only when all these aspects work in concert can we fully understand a given situation and respond appropriately. If they are not in concert, we get disharmony in our communications, which can spiral out of control and dive into negative realms.

Further to this it's important to realise that before we can understand anyone else, it's vital we understand ourselves. And we can gain self-understanding by engaging with ourselves, with our own inner thoughts and feelings, questioning where they came from and what they're about – and then we can start to begin to know ourselves.

Then, when in communications with others, you can engage your own positive self-talk, which will assist with controlling the communications and gaining understanding.

the Shower, the Course & the Thought Bubble

the Shower, the Course & the Thought Bubble

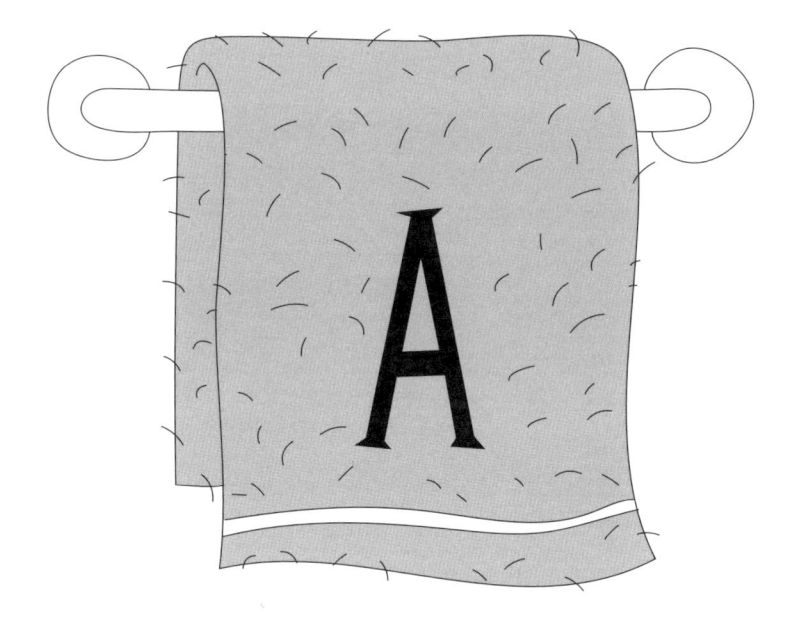

the Shower, the Course & the Thought Bubble

the Shower, the Course & the Thought Bubble

FpartOUR

I turned back to the white board and wrote A under the E, Q and U. "And once you understand," I said, "you can take the appropriate…"

"ACTION" came the answer loud and clear from all in the room.

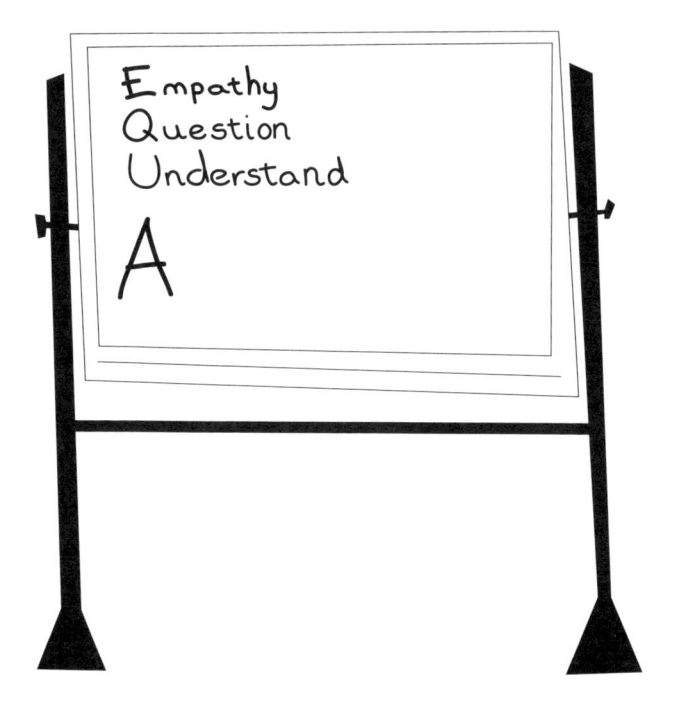

```
Empathy
Question
Understand
A
```

the Shower, the Course & the Thought Bubble

As I turned back from the white board I noticed Broad Grin Two mouthing the words, "I love the night life, I like to boogie…" while doing a bit of a chair dance. Broad Grin One seemed to catch the beat and they high fived, then settled once again.

"Okay. Action." I stated.

"What's so important about taking action?"

"Well if you don't, nothing happens," said the Expensive Suit Guy.

"True," I mused, "but what kind of action?"

"Action that's going to get you results," said Eighties Guy.

"Which is…?"

"Proactive?" he ventured.

"Yes," I replied, "but before we take any action we need to have undertaken the E, the Q and most importantly the U. Without empathy or questioning we have no understanding, which means that nine times out of ten our actions won't be correct."

(It was at this point that I had a quick chat to all the fellas in the house: "We as men are programmed to take action. It's not our fault, it's in our DNA – I am man, I hunt, I kill I do – that's our nature, it's the way we are programmed. But in these modern times we must hold ourselves back before we take action to ensure we take the correct action. And before we take any action the most important thing to do is centre ourselves, not just us guys but all of us.")

"What do you mean by that? Get all hippy and

the Shower, the Course & the Thought Bubble

start chanting or something?" queried Miss Negative in a surprisingly uplifted tone.

"No, No" I replied. "I mean – we need to grab hold of our reactions or our inner child (the ID), and think before we speak. The action I believe we need to take is appropriate, assertive action."

"What's assertive action?" asked Miss Negative. "Is it hitting someone?"

"No, that would be an aggressive action," I replied. "That is to behave in such a way that we violate the rights and feelings of others, which will usually lead to the other person being aggressive back to us and before you know it, it has lead to physical or verbal abuse by both parties."

"On the other hand," I continued, "being assertive is controlling your actions while being firm – it's saying what you need to say without being confrontational or argumentative. Assertiveness also allows you freedom to express what you need to, thereby ensuring you're not repressing whatever it is you need to get out of your system. Repression of any kind is a killer. Think of the word disease, this is in fact two words dis-ease and when we are uneasy with ourselves we get sick."

"So being assertive, even though it might be difficult at first, is very, very good for your health and the health of all who deal with you," I concluded.

"So how do we get to be assertive then?" asked the Now-Not-So-Shy Guy.

"By making a conscious decision to behave in

an assertive manner and practising it until it becomes second nature it will, as the result of being assertive, encourage us to be more assertive. It's like a positive spiral effect – the more you do it the better you feel and the more you want to do it – then others will treat us differently, more positively."

"So how do you do it?" he asked again.

"Well each person has to find their own way of doing it. I can only tell you what works for me," I responded.

"And what works for you," said Broad Grin One with an especially broad grin and a wink.

"I talk to my cat," I said. " Yep, straight up every morning, I get up, get dressed and before I leave the house I ask my cat what kind of day I am going to have and my cat (who can talk, true it's by telepathy) tells me I'm going to have a great day and that I'm going to enjoy meeting new people, enjoy the tram ride, the car drive whatever. He's a great cat, always gives me a feeling of positivity and wellbeing before demanding food. I have learned to talk to my cat before I feed him, otherwise he's not interested in me, just his bowl of food."

"So how does that help?" asked Sci-fi Girl.

"He centres me and gives me a positive spin on the day. I feel grounded and it gives me a base to work from, so no matter what happens when I walk out the door, at least I start the day in a positive frame of mind. That way as the day unfolds I am better prepared to deal with it and all the people that will come into my day."

"My boat's a bit like that," said The Voice. "Every time I get pissed off with life I go look at my boat and imagine being out at sea on a sunny day. I calm down and feel much better, it beats doing what I used to do, which was down a six pack and turn into an arsehole."

"I go dancing," chimed in Broad Grin Two.

"And I go to the gym," said Broad Grin One.

"These are all excellent techniques, but the one difference between what I am talking about and the strategies just mentioned is when I talk to my cat

I'm in a natural state of mind and I do it every day rather than as a reaction to something. Behaving out of reaction does not make us assertive," I stated.

"I get it," said the Woman-with-the-twelve-year-old. "It's like creating a positive state of mind for yourself – it's my life and I want to live it in a positive way. Like when my kids say they are bored on school holidays and I say to them 'boredom is a state of mind'. Then once I've taken positive action and made them laugh and we get into an activity time flies, because if I give in and say yes it is boring, the day drags and I end up going mad and shouting at them all day."

"Are you really saying that talking to your cat or having a laugh with your kids can change the way people treat you or the realities of life?" asked Expensive Suit Guy.

"Do you play any sport?" I queried.

"Not now, but I used to be a fair football player back in the day. I played semi-professional for a few seasons but then got injured and had to give it up for a season and never really got back into it," he said.

"Did you warm up before a training session or a match?" I asked.

"Yes of course I did, I'm not an idiot you know," he said.

"What was the main purpose of the warm up?" I asked.

"To prepare my body, especially if it was going to be a tough match. You go out onto a footy oval without a good warm-up and you'll be off with a serious injury within minutes," he said.

"What causes the injury?" I asked.

"Could be anything, but essentially your ligaments and tendons need to stretch. There are over 600 skeletal muscles attached directly or indirectly via the tendons to your bones and the ligaments hold your joints together," he replied. "Without a good warm-up, its like getting into a car and revving it up to the point of redlining it, then taking off really fast to find that you've got no oil. The engine will seize up and die. Well it's the same for the human body."

the Shower, the Course & the Thought Bubble

"Is the human mind not part of the human body?" I asked.

"Oh yes, I guess so," he said.

I could tell by the look on his face he knew what I was about to say.

"Okay, okay," he sighed. "I get it. "What you're saying is that warming up for your day is the same as warming up for a footy match, right?"

"Yes," I said, "except a footy match goes for a couple of hours in a confined space where you can openly see your opponents and everyone more or less plays by the established rules of the game. But in this thing we call life, rules are often determined by people's frame of mind or attitude in that moment in time."

I had the room's complete attention, so I continued.

"So it is even more important to warm yourself and your attitude up for the day. We can also change other people's states of mind by the way we behave. When we are centred and happy in ourselves and smile, other people who are not in that frame of mind can warm to us as we make them feel good about themselves by being warm, open and real."

"I know what you mean by that," said Expensive Suit Guy. "The other day I woke up in a really good mood for no apparent reason, got in my car to go to work, was happy vibing along, got to an intersection where I normally have to wait forever-and-a-day to join the main road. But not on this day – I smiled and was happy to wait, but this guy just let me in and then a little further up the road there was a car with a woman who was so stressed out I could feel her energy radiating from inside her car – so I let her in and I could see that little act of kindness on my part changed her whole mood! She smiled and waved thanks and I literally saw some of the tension fall away[8]."

Then Expensive Suit Guy said, "I decided that for the rest of the day I was going to be in a good mood and be generous to everyone. I had the best day ever. Most people were really happy to see me and behaved positively back to me and those that didn't I didn't worry about and let it go. Normally I would have got all stressed out, been aggressive towards them and ended up in a verbal fight. That's it I'm going to remember that day and see if I can do that every day. I might even get a cat," he mused.

"What would you call it?" asked The Voice.

"Cat of course, like on Red Dwarf," Sci-fi Girl answered before Expensive Suit Guy could get another word in.

---

8. We all have an energy field that surrounds us, called an aura. It changes colour depending on our mood and or state of health and can be measured or even photographed.

Everyone laughed.

"Laughter is also very good for you as it releases all these natural drugs into your system called endorphins and they actually make you feel uplifted and positive," said broad Grin Two.

"Let me get this straight then," said the Young Woman with the Impressive Mane. "Taking assertive action requires practise to get used to it, you usually get a positive response so you want to do it more, people can still be rude to you, but rather than getting all upset by that you let it go and stay in control of yourself while being centred and happy."

"In a nutshell that's it, Weebles wobble but they don't fall down," I sang. I could now see that they all thought I'd finally lost it.

"When I was a child I had this toy. It was egg shaped, it had a lead base (which accounts for my madness), and a hollow plastic upper section and the TV ad for the toy was 'Weebles wobble but they don't' fall down'." I explained.

"No matter which way you pushed a Weeble it always righted itself back to a standing position because the weight at the base gave it a centre of gravity and balanced the toy."

"Being an assertive human being means we have a base to stay centred. Most people wish to unbalance us so they can manipulate us into negative behaviours for their own ends. Assertive action turns us into confident, strong, open, friendly people who are easy to deal with because we are consistent and stable," I concluded.

"I like this, I really like this," said the former Ms Negative. "I can choose to be negative or I can choose to be positive and it's my choice, no one else's. Mine, all mine I can control my life and my destiny!"

note to readers: ACTION

The best type of action is appropriate action.

Appropriate action is assertive, well-thought out and has a strategy behind it. It is formulated from employing empathy, asking questions and gaining understanding. Then we take action.

Note to men: we need to remember that action is number four in the philosophy – not number one (despite instincts telling you to go and be an Action Hero without really thinking about it too much).

I'll clarify this in a romantic context: you're in a potential situation and you, being a man, tend to act on your romantic notion without putting too much thought into what your partner may need or want in order to respond to you. Here I must stress to you: don't take action until going through all the preceding steps. Because without taking the steps, how do you know whether to go don the superhero outfit or turn up with chocolates, flowers and ready to give a foot massage? You don't!

While men tend to take action without thinking, many women hang back from taking action because of a lack of assertiveness in their nature. Being assertive comes from being fully versed in a situation, which gives you control and the ability to speak out and act with confidence.

So remember, before taking action:

Gain empathy

Ask questions

Ensure you have a complete understanding

And only then will you have the tools to formulate a strategy for action and it will be the appropriate action to take.

the Shower, the Course & the Thought Bubble

the Shower, the Course & the Thought Bubble

the Shower, the Course & the Thought Bubble

ptart
FIVE

I turned back to the whiteboard and under the 'E-Q-U-A' I added an 'L'.

```
Empathy
Question
Understand
Action
L
```

"So the last one," I said. "Any takers?"

"Live," offered the now Ms Positive.

"I like it, but it's not the one I'm looking for."

"Love" said Broad Grin One.

"Another very good guess and EQUAL will definitely help you with your love life but it's not the word I need right now," I answered.

"Learn," said the guy who at the start of the afternoon was really shy, but now his tone and body language was of someone who was in control and confident.

"Excellent. But again not the word I'm after," I responded.

"Anyone else?" I asked, looking around the room.

I heard the word "link" come from the woman with the twelve-year old daughter.

"Curious," I said. "What made you think of link?"

"Well link is about communication and relationships between people," she replied.

"I like that very much," I said. "But no, it's still

not what I am looking for."

I wrote an E next to the L.

"Leverage," Eighties Man offered. His voice, I now noticed, was much quieter than it had been at the start of the session.

"I can see where you're coming from," I said to him, "but again it's not what I'm looking for."

Still no one got it, so I wrote an A next to the L and the E.

As I looked around the room I could see a collective moment where it dawned on the group almost simultaneously and I heard the word I was looking for loud and strong from everyone.

"LEAD", they said.

It's "LEAD!"

I smiled and asked how they knew it would be the word lead.

"Well it just makes sense," responded Sci-fi Girl. "All the things we have been talking about require us to lead the communication,"

"And our attitude," came The Voice.

"As well as our behaviour," said the Young Woman with the Impressive Mane.

"True," I said. "Leading is much more than just being in control, it's about making an active choice."

"I think it's about leading your life," said the Guy in the Expensive Suit. "I mean, we hear the term all the time in the past tense but rarely apply it to the here and now."

"What do you mean?" I asked.

"Well, I was at a funeral the other day, a friend of my dad had died, and the church minister bloke was going on about how this guy had lead a good life blah, blah … and I was thinking to myself, 'no he didn't, my dad's friend hadn't really lead his life at all. He was a weak kind of guy who just went with the flow, never really had an opinion of his own, just followed the crowd and did whatever the others in the group did'," he replied.

"I now see to lead your life requires courage and self-leadership. It's like you need to be your own footy coach or something," said Expensive Suit Guy.

"And there was me thinking of getting a personal trainer at eighty dollars an hour! Now I see I can be my own personal trainer by making a real choice about my life and what I want to do with it, including staying fit," said the Woman with the Impressive Mane.

"Once we know where we are coming from and what we want, that kind of turns us into a natural leader, especially if we are being a grown up or using emotional intelligence," offered The Voice.

"Yes," I said, "it does."

"It's a bit like my boat," continued The Voice. "A boat without a rudder, a sail or an engine will just drift along at the mercy of the wind, waves and tide. But a boat with a rudder, sail and engine can create its direction, giving the captain of the boat (me in this case) control and choice."

"Man, that's so Jean Luc Picard," said Sci-fi Girl. "That's the way he runs the Enterprise. He always has the best interests of his crew foremost in his mind, he empathises (with the help of an empath), then he consults his senior officers and asks them questions (usually open). He then understands the situation, takes assertive action and leads his crew. Way cool - Star Trek meets EQUAL."

"So what you're saying is," said Eighties Man, "see all things from other people's points of view … gain empathy by asking open questions and confirm with closed questions, which will now give you an understanding of what they are really thinking. Then take the appropriate action for the best results. Having the courage to lead your communications in this way will mean that in the end you are happier, less stressed and have better relationships at work, home and in the world in general."

"Nicely put," I said to Eighties Man. "Thanks for the summary."

"Well I just don't believe it for one minute and I don't think anyone else does either," he said.

"Speak for yourself," said the Not-Shy-At-All-

Any-More-Guy. "Just because you don't believe it doesn't make it untrue."

"It's the same with crop circles[9]. They appear all over the world, particularly in England. They're massive, complex designs, geometrically perfect, formed in fields from bent (not broken) crops usually within minutes without a single ear of corn or whatever crop being damaged and people have the same reaction as you do. They can see it yet they refuse to believe it," he said to Eighties Man.

"I don't think it's a question of believing, I think it's a question of doing," said the Woman-with-the-Twelve-Year-Old. "As a mum I already do most of this with my kids unconsciously and now I want to do it with everyone consciously! I want to live a life that's mine – with direction, purpose and clear communication with as many people as I can – because I know I will get more out of my time in this world if I do," she said emphatically.

"Misunderstanding and miscommunication

---
9. Crop circles - see Secrets in the Fields by Freddy Silva.

leads to stress and stress leads to dis-ease and disease leads to an early death and I'm not going there," she concluded.

"Right on, I'm with you sister," called out Broad Grin Two. "I don't have kids, probably never will, I am what and who I am and proud to be so, and can now hold my ground, particularly if I can be a grown up about things and understand that people say and do things based more on their own emotions rather than who I am."

At this, Broad Grin One leaned over, took Broad Grin Two by the hand and said, "next time my manager tries to intimidate me, boy is she in for a shock. This Weeble may wobble but she ain't gonna fall down, she's my dog now."

They looked at each other with genuine smiles and I could see the camaraderie and support for each other was strong.

"Now I understand that leadership is not negative or about trying to get people to 'do as I say', but it's about choice – personal choice. Everything in life we do or say has ramifications," said Expensive Suit Guy.

"Yes that's it," I replied. "The action you take now becomes your past and creates your future. You have to deal with the consequences of whatever you do or say."

"I think at the end of the day it's important for us to remember that we're all responsible for ourselves, our thoughts and our actions," I said. "After all, it's our thoughts, actions and behaviours that create the place that we live in and, some would say, who we are, as we are made up of around 70 percent water (the planet is covered by 70 percent water)."

"Water has been proved by Doctor Emoto[10] to change depending on how it is treated. Water that has been talked to, respected and thought about in a positive manner will create healthier crystalline structures than water that has had negative input," I said.

---

10. Dr. Masaru Emoto's Messages in Water were popularised in the 2004 documentary film What the Bleep do we Know.

the Shower, the Course & the Thought Bubble

I noticed the time was now ten to five.

"Okay," I said. "We're almost out of time. Any questions or comments before I draw the course to a close?"

"Yes," said Eighties Man. "This all sounds terrific now, but who's going to believe it or practice it outside this room? I bet everyone here –"

"There you go again, talking for the group" interjected the now Ms Very Positive.

"– will forget the whole thing by this time next week and go back to doing the same things they were and thinking in the same old way," he continued.

"Is the earth round like a football[11] or flat like a plate?" I asked Eighties Man.

"Round of course, everyone knows that," he answered.

---

11. Just in case you are thinking that footballs are an oval shape, let me put this straight. Footballs are a round, spherical shape. Rugby balls, Australian Rules footballs or American gridiron balls are all oval, but these games are not the WORLD GAME, which is football, sometimes known as soccer. The word soccer was an abbreviation from association (from assoc.) and is said to have first been coined in the 1880s. In 2004 the term football became the official name for soccer in Australia.

the Shower, the Course & the Thought Bubble

"Has the world always been round?"

"Yes, but some people thought it was flat," he said.

"Not some people" said The Voice. "Everyone thought so, except for a few great thinkers like Aristarchus; he was around at about the same time as Aristotle. Aristotle thought that the universe revolved around the earth and the earth was a flat disk at the centre of the universe. I guess most people liked the idea that we were the centre of everything so chose to go with his theories."

"Then along came Nicolas Copernicus (1473-1543), and he changed it all," concluded The Voice's lesson.

the Shower, the Course & the Thought Bubble

"I remember him from my history classes," said a beaming Broad Grin One. "He made the point that we are not the centre of the universe – the sun is – and we revolve around the sun along with all the other planets."

"Indeed he did" I agreed, "and do you think that his message was well received and everyone just went 'oh okay, the world is round now'."

"No way!" responded Broad Grin One. "People were tortured, even killed, for believing in what Copernicus had written. Galileo spent the rest of his life in prison after talking about Copernicus's theories."

Sitting back all smug in his chair, Eighties Man now said, "so, are you saying we're now all going to be tortured and killed for going back to work and talking about EQUAL? It's not like this will change the course of human history or anything. Is it?"

"Maybe, maybe not" I replied. "But I do know this: any new idea or way of thinking will meet with resistance and the better the idea the

the Shower, the Course & the Thought Bubble

greater the resistance. After all, if the way someone is communicating with you gives them power over you they are not going to want their power reduced, so they will do and say many things in order to ensure they keep the status quo, even if they can quite clearly see their actions will bring about destruction."

Suddenly Sci-fi Girl was on her feet. "It's like in Star Wars Three when Chancellor Palpatine says to Anakin Skywalker, 'all who have power are afraid to lose their power'."

"Exactly," I said. "But over time the truth becomes self-evident and widespread and can no longer be hidden or explained away and the paradigm shifts."

"If humankind is to continue we must evolve, we must grow, become emotionally intelligent, respect each other, respect the planet we live on and change the way we do business and our way of communicating with each other. I believe that EQUAL is part of this movement," chimed in Not-Shy-At-All-Guy.

We all turned to look at him, completely taken aback by how powerfully he spoke.

Very pleased, I turned to the group and concluded the session.

"Meet resistance with emotional intelligence and know that the resistance will fade, just like the notion of a flat earth faded. True, not everyone will evolve with us (even today there are some who still believe and passionately argue that the earth is still flat, but they are few in number[12]), but our numbers are growing and becoming stronger."

As Sci-fi Girl would point out: it is fear, anger

---

12. Refer to The Flat Earth Society – http://www.theflatearthsociety.org

and hate that lead to the dark side of the force[13].

So go on, be brave and give EQUAL a chance to change your life and more importantly change the lives of the people around you.

That's living in the light, it is not always easy but it is always worth doing.

EQUALISE IT!

And with that the course had ended and EQUAL was indeed proven.

---

13. Star Wars Episode 1: The Phantom Menace, © 2005 Lucasfilm Ltd & TM

the Shower, the Course & the Thought Bubble

note to readers: LEAD

If you're not leading, somebody else is. So it's your choice to consciously lead your own life and all that happens within it, because if you don't, then you're subconsciously choosing to be lead by somebody else.

While our past experiences are always with us, we're not imprisoned within them. We do however become creatures of habit – which isn't a bad thing if you have good habits. Once again, it's the choices you make that determine your habits as well.

How this relates to leading, is that leading is habitual behaviour and that is a very positive habit to invest in, especially because true leaders are fully informed about the situation or person they are leading because they have empathised, questioned, understood and taken appropriate action, which is the

the Shower, the Course & the Thought Bubble

key to achieving the best results and being a good leader.

the Shower, the Course & the Thought Bubble

the Shower, the Course & the Thought Bubble

Six part

E-Q-U-A-L

Empathy
Question
Understand
Action
Lead

I hope you've enjoyed reading this book and that the principles and tips throughout it will help you in all your communications throughout your life.

the Shower, the Course & the Thought Bubble

Equal is a communications tool that I have used since that moment in the shower all those years ago. Since workshopping it during the training session used as the basis for this book, it has assisted me in all my communications since – and will keep doing so.

Now, after reading *The Shower, The Course and The Thought Bubble*, you will have a tool you can use to have constructive, meaningful communications in all aspects of your life.

I sincerely believe you will now use the principle. It is your choice – you can choose to apply the information and develop positive life habits, or remain in your current habits.

E
Q
U   **It's a great way to grasp life!**
A
L

the Shower, the Course & the Thought Bubble

Now here's a whole new book!

>**G**row
>
>**R**elate
>
>**A**spire
>
>**S**erve
>
>**P**rosper

Hmmmm…

>Enjoy,
>
>*Rum Charles*

INDIGO TRAINING

To find out more about Rum Charles or Indigo Training please go to:

www.indigotraining.com.au

Email: Info@indigotraining.com.au
and to contact Rum Charles directly
rum@indigotraining.com.au

Or if you would like to call us
our phone number is 03 9820 0277.

ORDER

                                                                QTY

**The Shower, the Course & the
   Thought Bubble** $22.99   ....

Postage within Australia (1 book) $5.00   ....
Postage within Australia (2 or more books) $9.00   ....

                                    TOTAL* $_____
                                    * All prices include GST

Name: ....

Address: ....

Phone: ....

Email Address: ....

Payment:

❑ Money Order ❑ Cheque ❑ Amex ❑ MasterCard ❑ Visa

Cardholder's Name:..

Credit Card Number: ....

Signature:...

Expiry Date: ....

Allow 21 days for delivery.

Payment to: Better Bookshop (ABN 14 067 257 390)
              PO Box 12544
              A'Beckett Street, Melbourne, 8006
              Victoria, Australia
              Fax: +61 3 9671 4730
              betterbookshop@brolgapublishing.com.au

BE PUBLISHED

Publishing through a successful Australian publisher. Brolga provides:
- Editorial appraisal
- Cover design
- Typesetting
- Printing
- Author promotion
- National book trade distribution, including sales, marketing and distribution through Macmillan Australia.

For details and inquiries, contact:
Brolga Publishing Pty Ltd
PO Box 12544
A'Beckett St VIC 8006

Phone: 03 9662 2633
Fax: 03 9671 4730
bepublished@brolgapublishing.com.au
markzocchi@brolgapublishing.com.au
ABN: 46 063 962 443